D1123622

Sadler, Wendy.
Using ramps and wedges /
c2005.
33305211503036
ca   11/07/06

de Machines

Using Ramps and Wedges

Wendy Sadler

Raintree

Chicago, Illinois

© 2005 Raintree
Published by Raintree, a division of Reed Elsevier Inc.
Chicago, IL 60602
Customer Service 888-363-4266
Visit our website at www.raintreelibrary.com

All rights reserved. No part of this publication may be reproduced or transmitted in any form or by any means, electronic or mechanical, including photography, recording, taping, or any information storage and retrieval system, without permission in writing from the publishers.

For information address the publisher:
Raintree, 100 N. LaSalle, Suite 1200, Chicago, IL 60602

Printed and bound in China by South China Printing Company

09 08 07 06 05
10 9 8 7 6 5 4 3 2 1

Library of Congress Cataloging-in-Publication Data:
Cataloging-in-Publication Data is on file at the Library of Congress.

ISBN 1-4109-1447-X (lib. binding), 1-4109-1454-2 (Pbk.)

Acknowledgments
The publishers would like to thank the following for permission to reproduce photographs:
Alamy Images (Photofusion Picture Library) p. 10; Corbis pp. 17, 28; Corbis (Sygma/ Daemmrich Bob) p. 9; Corbis (Amos Nachoum) p. 26; Corbis (Bo Zaunders) p. 4; Corbis (Bruce Miller) p. 25; Corbis (David Aubrey) p. 20; Corbis (Gunter Marx) p. 24; Corbis (Lester Lefkowitz) p. 14; Corbis (NewSport) p. 5; Corbis (Raymond Gehman) p. 19; Getty Images (Imagebank) pp. 27, 29; Getty Images/Stone p. 11; Harcourt Education Ltd (Tudor Photography) pp. 6, 8, 12, 15, 16, 18, 21, 22; REX Features pp. 7, 13.

Cover photograph of zipper reproduced with permission of Getty Images (The Image Bank)

Every effort has been made to contact copyright holders of any material reproduced in this book. Any omissions will be rectified in subsequent printings if notice is given to the publishers.

Disclaimer:
All the Internet addresses (URLs) given in this book were valid at the time of going to press. However, due to the dynamic nature of the Internet, some addresses may have changed, or sites may have changed or ceased to exist since publication. While the author and publishers regret any inconvenience this may cause readers, no responsibility for any such changes can be accepted by either the author or the publishers.

Contents

Any words appearing in the text in bold,
like this, are explained in the glossary.

Machines with Ramps and Wedges

If you look around you every day, you can see ramps and **wedges** in action. Cars are driven onto ferries using ramps. Airplanes are held in place at the airport using wedges behind the wheels. You use two wedges when you cut paper using scissors.

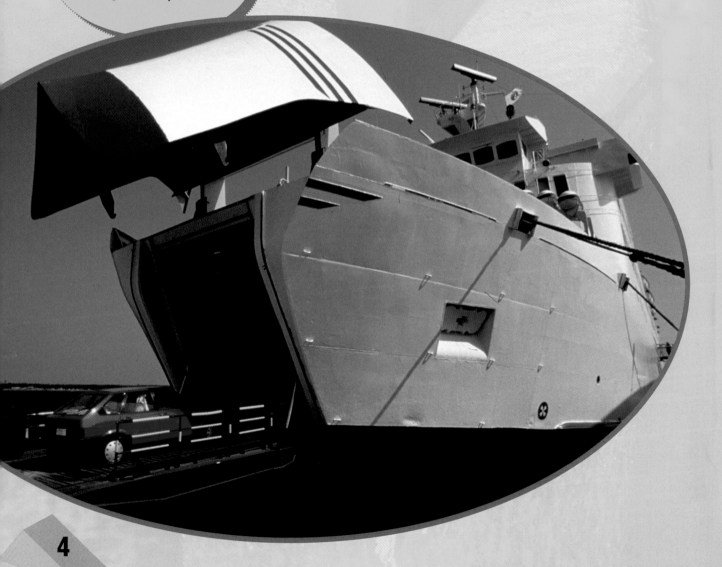

This car is being driven onto a ferry using a ramp.

People who play golf use clubs called wedges. The shape of these clubs helps push the ball and lift it up into the air at the same time.

Ramps and wedges are both **slopes** that help us do things. They are very simple, but very important.

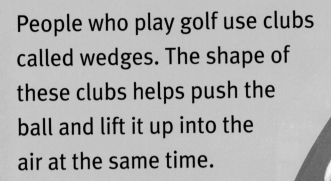

Wedges are used in golf to lift the ball up into the air.

What Is a Ramp?

A ramp is a **simple machine** that helps us to move things in a **vertical** direction (up or down). A ramp is a **slope,** which means it is a flat surface that has one end higher than the other.

A ramp makes an **angle** with the ground like the corner of a triangle. Ramps are also called **inclined planes.**

A skateboard rolls easily up and down a ramp.

6

Imagine trying to slide a heavy box up a ramp. It would be very difficult because the box and the ramp would rub together. This rubbing is a **force** called **friction.** It makes it harder to push the box up the slope. If some wheels were added to the box, there would be much less friction. This means it would be easier to move the box up the ramp.

These boxes have been put on a cart. The cart has wheels that make it easier to pull the boxes up the ramp.

Activity

Put the palms of your hands together and rub them back and forth as fast as you can. There is friction between your hands. What does it feel like?

How Do Ramps Help Us?

When you need to move something, it takes work. The work required is a mixture of the **effort force** you put in and the distance you want the object to move.

Effort force is how much you have to push or pull. If you need to lift a heavy box straight up in the air, you move it only a small distance. Still, you need to use a lot of effort force, because it is so heavy.

Lifting a heavy box can be very hard to do and can be dangerous even for adults. You should never lift overly heavy boxes.

When you use a ramp, you move the box a longer distance because the length of the **slope** is more than the height of the ramp. You have to push the box farther, but the effort force you use is less. This makes the job a lot easier. A longer ramp will make the slope less steep, which makes the job even easier to do.

height of ramp

length of slope

The length of the slope is bigger than the height you need to lift the heavy object.

Ramps All Around You

Some vehicles have ramps as well as steps up to the door. The ramp helps people using wheelchairs to get onto the vehicle.

The distance up a ramp is more than the distance up a set of steps, but because a ramp has a smooth **slope,** wheels can roll up it. A ramp cannot be too steep, or it would be too hard to get up and too fast coming down.

It would be very hard work trying to get a wheelchair onto this bus without a ramp.

Ramps in hills

San Francisco has lots of steep hills. Some of the hills are too steep for cars to drive straight up or down. One street uses ramps arranged in a zigzag pattern. This means you drive a longer distance to get to the top or bottom of the hill, but it is easier and safer to climb and descend this way.

These ramps make the cars drive a longer distance, but they make it easier and safer to drive up and down the hill.

11

Ramps in Machines

Not all ramps help you climb hills. On a hot day, they can also help you cool down. The blades on a fan are ramps. The ramps are joined onto a wheel and **axle** so that they can spin around. As they turn around, the ramps push air forward.

A fan is a **compound machine** because it uses at least two **simple machines** together.

If you look at a fan from the side, you can see the slopes of the blades.

When you go on an escalator, you are moving up or down a ramp. Stairs are a type of ramp as well, even though they do not a have a smooth **slope.** You travel a longer distance by going up stairs or an escalator, but you can climb very high. You could not possibly climb this distance with just one big step on your own!

An escalator carries you up or down a ramp without you climbing it yourself.

Ramps for Fun

The ramps on a roller coaster carry you quickly up and down over very large distances. Sometimes you are pulled up the first **slope** by wheels, **pulleys,** and an **engine.** Then, the **force** of **gravity** makes the roller coaster move downward.

A roller coaster uses ramps, wheels, and pulleys to give you an exciting ride!

If the roller coaster fell straight down, it would land with a very large bump. The ramps let the roller coaster move down more gently and safely.

Some unusual clocks use ramps to tell us the time. Metal balls roll down ramps inside the clock. Each ball takes a certain time to roll down the ramps. The number of balls at the bottom tells us how much time has gone by.

The ramps in this clock are important because they make the balls fall downward more slowly than if they were just dropped.

What Is a Wedge?

A ramp or **inclined plane** is usually placed on the ground. You use the **slope** to help you climb. It is the surface of the ramp that is important for the jobs it does.

A **wedge** is a different shape that looks like two solid ramps stuck together. A wedge usually does its job by pushing through something.

A wedge is a solid shape that looks like two ramps stuck together.

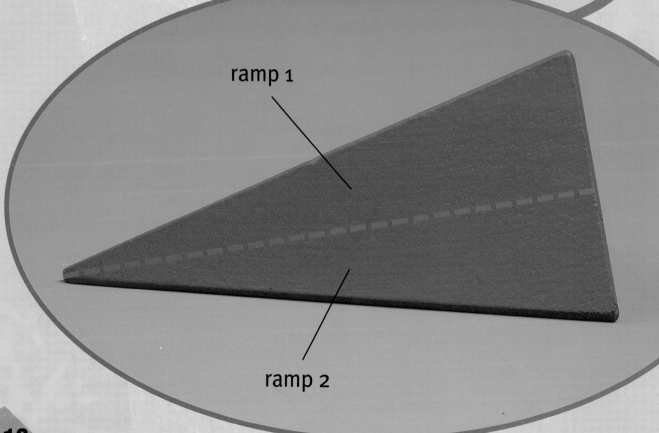

ramp 1

ramp 2

A wedge is a **simple machine** that helps to push things apart. By pushing the wide end of the wedge, it moves downward into some **material.** As the wedge moves through the material, the push downward turns into a push outward.

A wedge changes a forward or downward movement into an outward movement. This happens because the wide part of the wedge is now in the material and pushing it apart.

push downward

push outward

push outward

A hammer can be used to bash a wedge into something such as this tree trunk.

What Does a Wedge Do?

Wedges are usually used to push things apart. An ax has a metal head with one narrow, sharp end and one wide end. An ax can be used to cut wood, which is a hard **material.**

When you look at an ax head from above, you can see the wedge shape.

What would happen without . . . ?

The ax makes it possible for us to cut up trees. It would be almost impossible to cut open a tree trunk using just your hands.

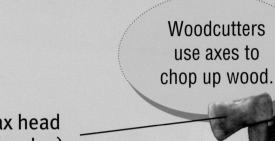
Woodcutters use axes to chop up wood.

ax head
(wedge)

handle
(lever)

The head of an ax is joined to a handle, which gives you something to hold on to. The handle is also a **lever.** A lever is another **simple machine.**

When you swing an ax, the ax head moves a larger distance than the handle where you hold it. This makes the ax head move faster, so it can cut into things. An ax is a **compound machine.** Again, a compound machine is something that uses two or more simple machines together.

Wedges in Everyday Life

Pins that hold up posters are also **wedges.** If you look at the pins closely, you can see that they become very narrow at the end. A pin or needle is a sort of round wedge. It does not have just two **slopes,** but it works in the same way as an ordinary wedge.

These pins are tiny wedges. Can you see the wedge shape?

What would happen without . . . ?

Without wedges in pins and needles, it would be a lot harder to push things into walls or through **material.** Imagine trying to push a pin without a sharp point on its end into a wall. Ouch!

A door wedge helps to hold a door open. When the door tries to close, it pushes against the wedge. The wedge shape pushes up against the bottom of the door and down against the floor. This means there is a lot of **friction** between the wedge, the door, and the floor. The wedge will not move, and the door stays open.

All the different pushes from the door and the wedge cause friction. This stops the door from moving.

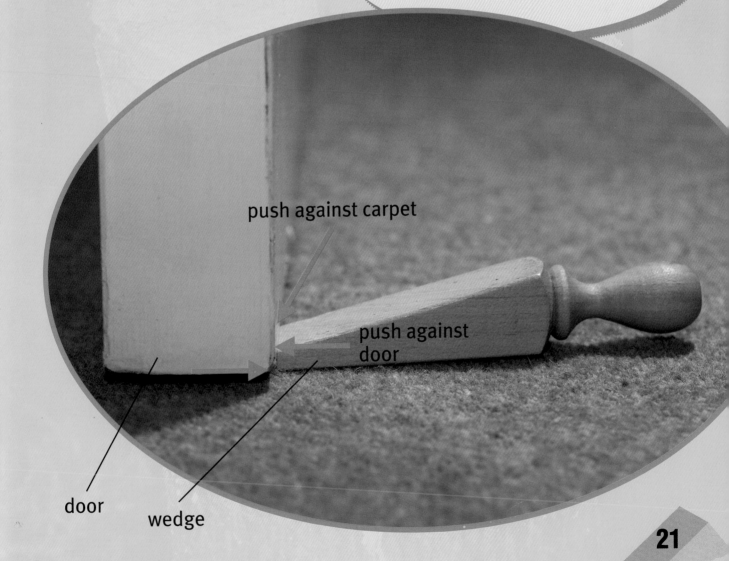

push against carpet

push against door

door

wedge

wearing wedges

A zipper is something that uses **wedges.** Look closely at a zipper on your clothes or on a bag. On either side of the zipper, you can see lots of small "teeth." These special shapes lock together to hold your clothes or bag shut.

The part of the zipper that you pull to join the teeth together is called the slide.

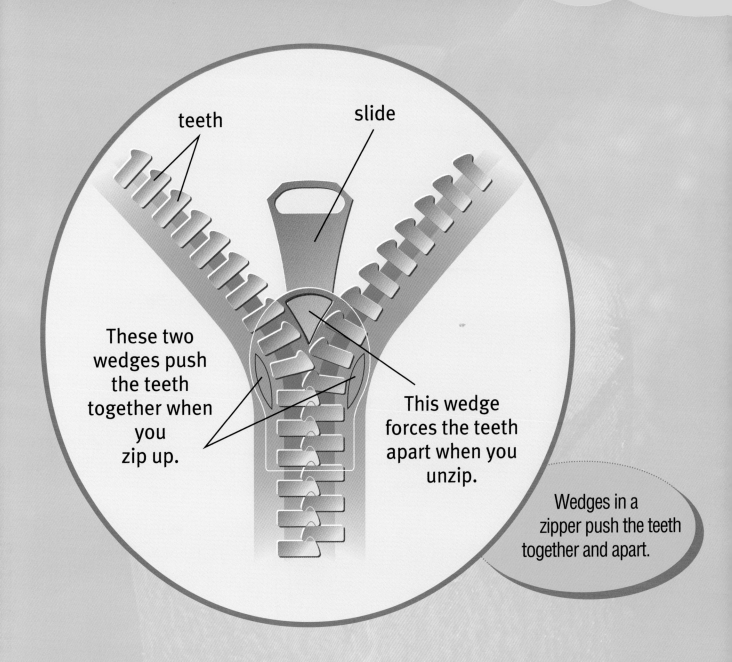

teeth

slide

These two wedges push the teeth together when you zip up.

This wedge forces the teeth apart when you unzip.

Wedges in a zipper push the teeth together and apart.

The slide of a zipper has three wedges inside it. The wedge at the top is triangle shaped. It is used to push the teeth apart when you pull the zipper down. The other two wedges are oval shaped. These wedges push the teeth together again when you pull the slide up. They make the two sides of the zipper lock together.

Wedges in Machines

Farmers use **wedges** in a machine called a plow. A plow has lots of blades that cut through soil. Each blade is a wedge. As a tractor pulls the plow, the sharp ends of the blades dig into the soil. The blades are also **sloped** like a ramp. This lifts the soil up and also pushes it apart.

tractor

plow

blade

Turning over all the soil in this field would be a tough job without the tractor and plow!

Boats and snowplows use a wedge shape at the front. This helps them travel through water or snow. The wedge helps them move with less **effort force** because it pushes the water or snow out to the side.

Speedboats use a wedge to help them travel through water very quickly.

What would happen without . . . ?

If a boat had a flat front, it would take a lot more effort force to move it through the water. It would not be able to go very quickly because the water would push right up against it.

A shark's teeth are **wedges.** Like humans, sharks push their teeth together to bite into food. Sharks' teeth have tiny blades along the edges that help them to tear up their food.

Sharks and other fish have wedge-shaped bodies to help them swim smoothly and quickly through water.

Your front teeth are also wedge shaped. Feel how they are thicker at the top and thinner at the bottom. Your teeth are shaped so that you can bite into hard foods and pull small pieces into your mouth.

The big square teeth at the back of your mouth are not so good for biting. They are for grinding up the food that is already in your mouth.

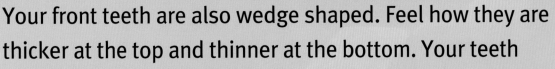

The wedges in your front teeth help to bite into hard foods such as apples.

Ramps and Wedges in Machines

The blades of a pair of scissors are two **wedges.** These blades are fixed together like two **levers** to make a machine that cuts things. The levers let you close the handles at one end of the scissors. As you do this, the blades close together. Your **effort force** on the handles becomes a pushing down **force** on the blades. The blades then push the paper apart.

joined together like levers

blades (wedges)

A pair of scissors uses wedges and levers together, so it is a **compound machine.**

If you make a ramp and wrap it around a pole, you get another very useful machine called a screw. When you turn a screw, the ramp around the screw's side helps you to move the screw slowly into a surface. A screw is a **simple machine** that turns turning movement into back and forth movement.

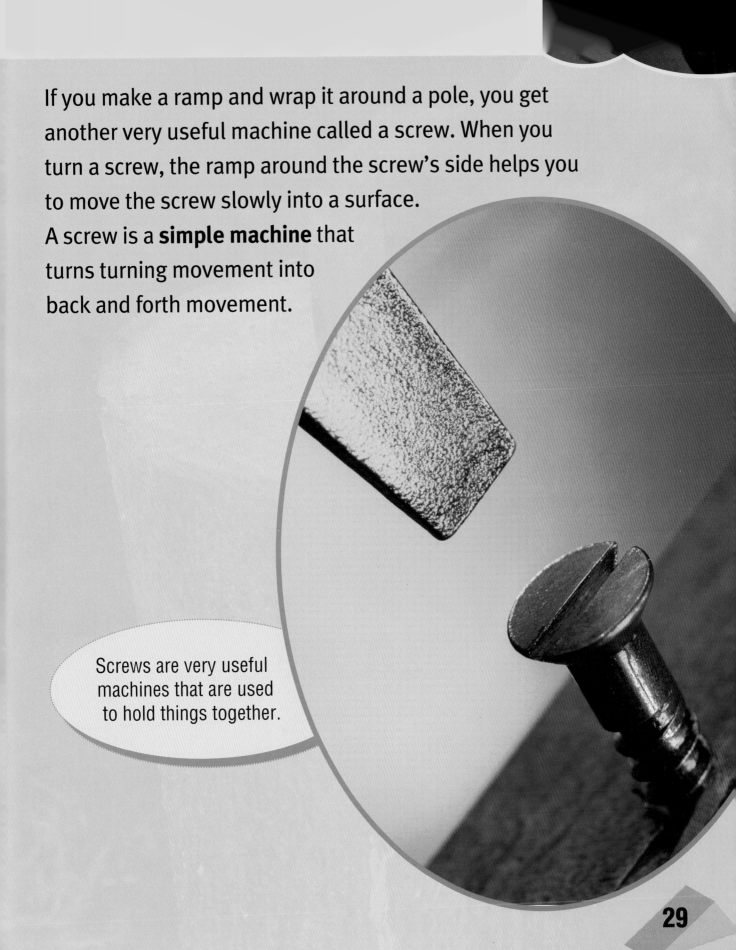

Screws are very useful machines that are used to hold things together.

Find Out for Yourself

You can find out about ramps and **wedges** by talking to your teacher or parents. Think about the **simple machines** you use every day. How do you think they work? Your local library will have books and information about this. You will find the answers to many of your questions in this book, but you can also use other books and the Internet.

Books to read

Douglas, Lloyd G. *What Is a Wedge?* Danbury, Conn.: Scholastic Library Publishing, 2003.

Oxlade, Chris. *Very Useful Machines: Ramps and Wedges*. Chicago, Ill.: Heinemann Library, 2003.

Using the Internet

Explore the Internet to find out more about ramps and wedges. Try using a search engine such as www.yahooligans.com or www.internet4kids.com, and type in keywords such as "ramp," "wedge," and **"slope."**

Glossary

angle   pointed space between two lines. The corner of an object.

axle   thin bar (rod) that goes through the center of a wheel or group of wheels

compound machine   machine that uses two or more simple machines

effort force   push or pull that you put into a ramp or wedge to move or lift something

engine   machine that can make things move

force   push or pull used to move or lift something

friction   something that happens when two surfaces rub against one another. Friction can slow things down or stop them from moving.

gravity   force in nature that pulls everything toward the ground

inclined plane   sloping surface or ramp

lever   stiff bar or stick that moves around a fixed point

material   substance that can be used to make things. Wood, brick, plastic, and paper are all examples of materials.

pulley   rope or chain wrapped around a wheel and axle to help lift things up

simple machine   something that can change the effort force (push or pull you provide) needed to move something or change the direction it moves

slope   flat surface with one end higher than the other

vertical   up and down

wedge   two ramps joined together, back to back

Index